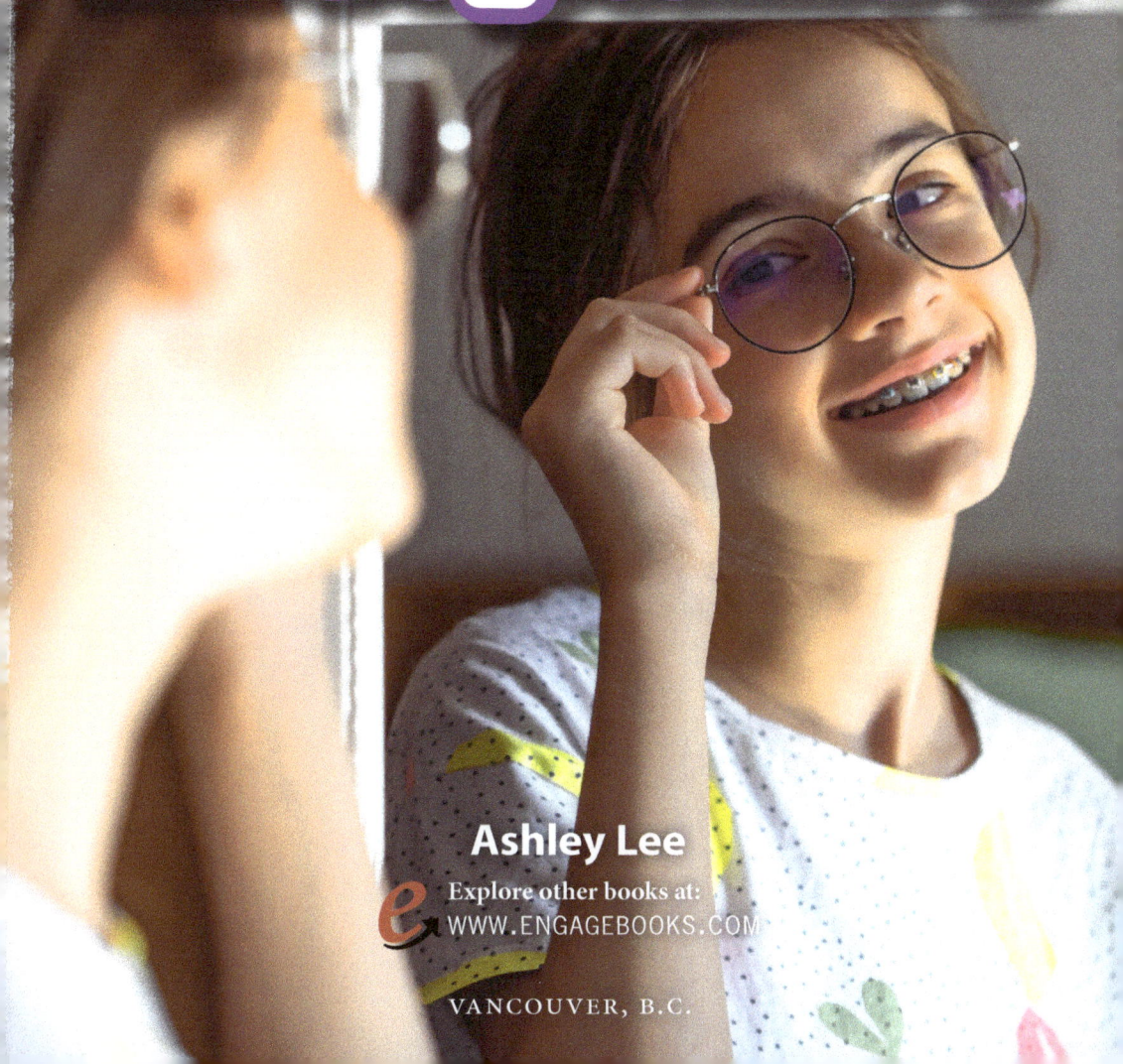

Good Character Traits

Acceptance

Ashley Lee

Explore other books at:
WWW.ENGAGEBOOKS.COM

VANCOUVER, B.C.

e WWW.ENGAGEBOOKS.COM

Acceptance: Good Character Traits
Lee, Ashley, 1995 –
Text © 2025 Engage Books
Design © 2025 Engage Books

Edited by: A.R. Roumanis
Design by: Mandy Christiansen

Text set in Myriad Pro Regular.
Chapter headings set in Anton.

FIRST EDITION / FIRST PRINTING

LIBRARY AND ARCHIVES CANADA CATALOGUING IN PUBLICATION

Title: Acceptance / Ashley Lee.
Names: Lee, Ashley, author.
Description: Series statement: Good Character Traits

ISBN 978-1-77878-734-8 (hardcover)
ISBN 978-1-77878-740-9 (softcover)

This project has been made possible in part by the Government of Canada.

Canada

Acceptance

Contents

What Is Acceptance?

Acceptance means being okay with the way things are. It means not **dwelling** on things that cannot be changed.

Key Word

Dwelling: thinking or talking about something a lot.

You can be accepting of other people or what is going on around you. You can also be accepting of your feelings.

Acceptance does not mean you have to be okay with someone's bad behavior.

Why Is Acceptance Important?

Accepting other people's differences helps make the world a kind place. It helps everyone get along.

Accepting what is going on around you helps you find ways to move forward. Accepting your feelings can stop you from feeling worse.

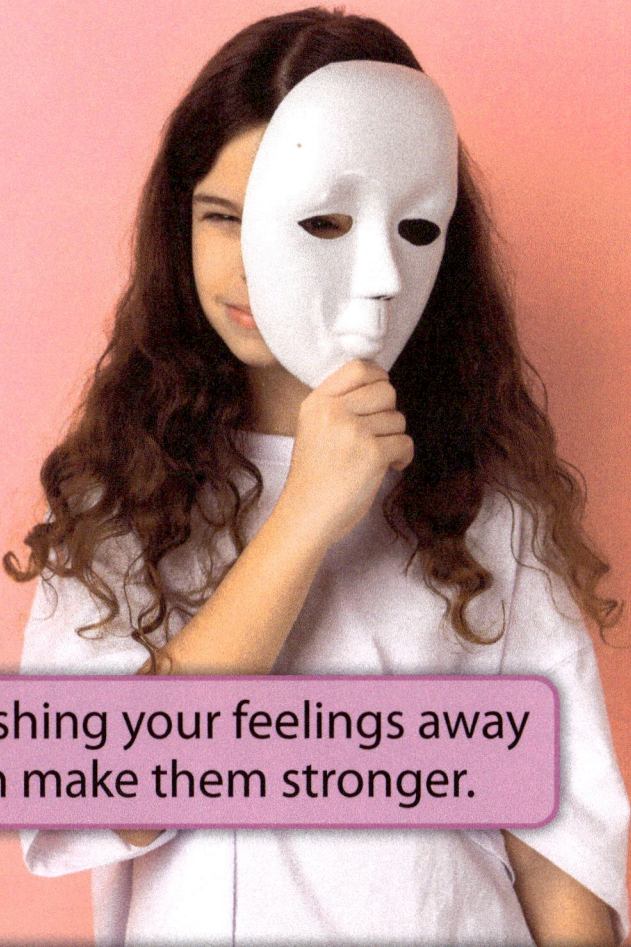

Pushing your feelings away can make them stronger.

What Does Acceptance Look Like?

People who accept others do not try to change them. People who accept the things around them look to the future instead of the past.

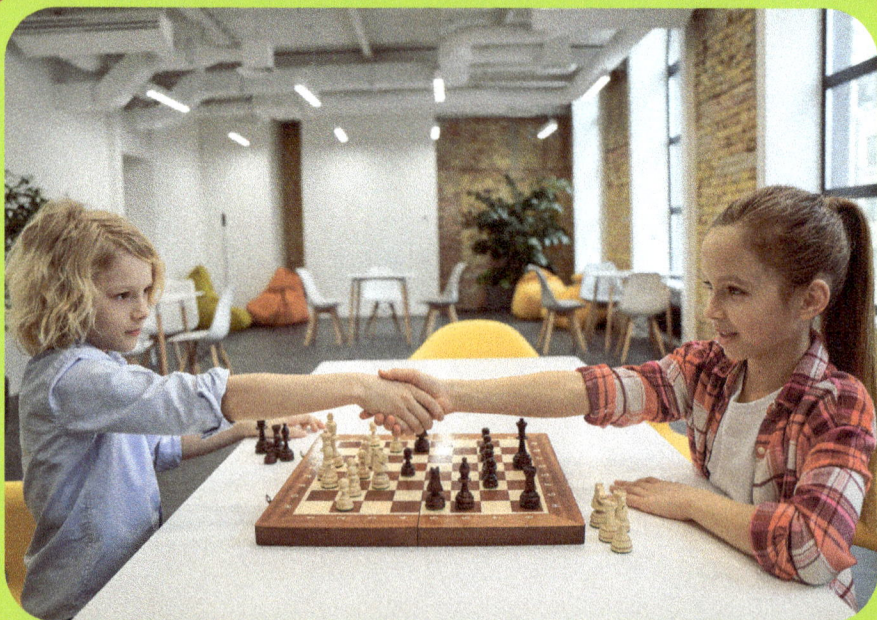

People who accept their feelings do not try to make themselves feel differently. They give themselves time to feel what they need to feel.

How Does Acceptance Affect You?

Acceptance helps you to think about good things instead of bad things. This can make you feel happier.

Acceptance also helps you feel calm. You no longer feel the need to fight to change things that cannot be changed.

How Does Acceptance Affect Others?

Accepting others can make them feel safe and happy. They know you will not **judge** them for being who they are.

Key Word

Judge: form an opinion depending on what you believe.

People who are accepted by others are more likely to feel good about themselves. They often like who they are.

Is Everyone Accepting?

Some people have a hard time accepting people who are different from them. Others have a hard time accepting themselves.

Some people have a hard time accepting when something bad happens. They might try to ignore it or **blame** everyone else for their problems.

Key Word

Blame: say or think that someone did something wrong.

Is It Bad if You Are Not Accepting?

It is okay to not be accepting of your feelings or what is going on around you sometimes. But you should always try to be accepting of other people.

It is important to be accepting of yourself as well as others.

It is okay if you forget sometimes. Just make sure to say sorry to the person you did not accept.

Does Acceptance Change Over Time?

Some people become more accepting as they get older. They learn that acceptance can make them happier.

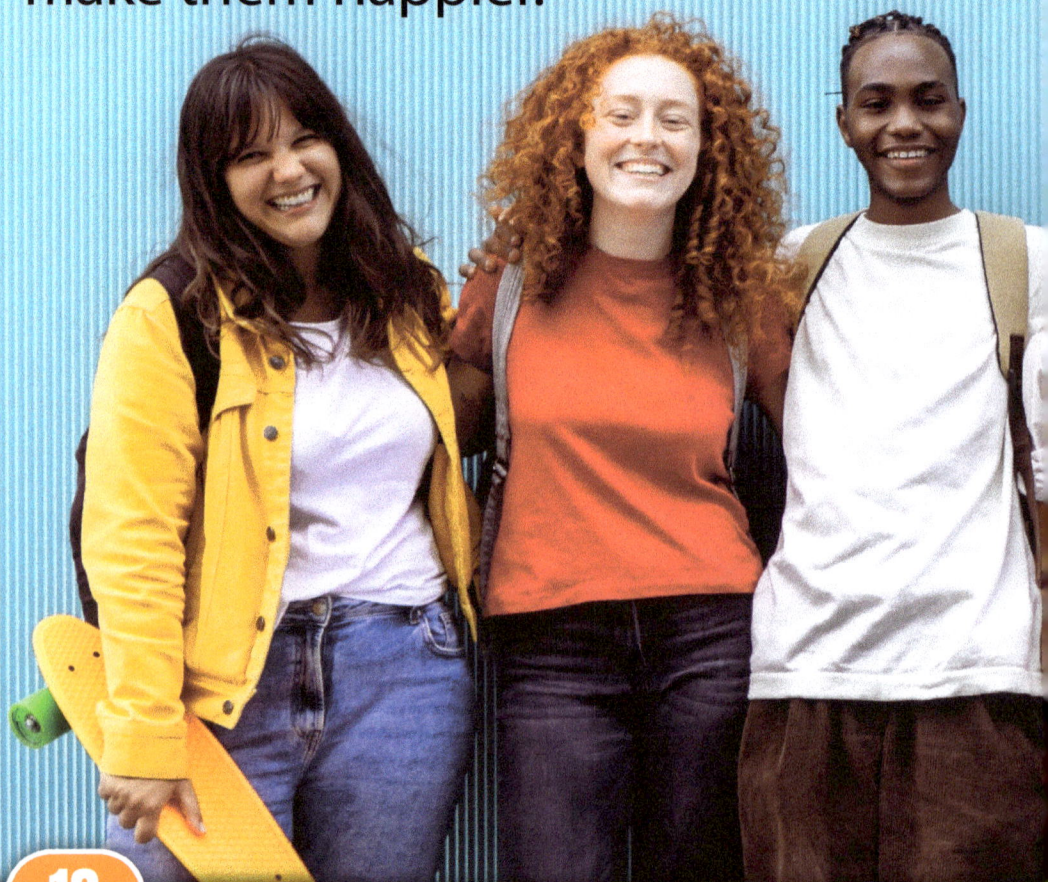

Some people become less accepting over time. They may be hurt that others do not accept them. This can make them think they are better than others.

Is It Hard to Be Accepting?

It can be hard to accept your feelings when you do not want to feel angry or sad. It can also be hard to be okay with something when you do not like it.

Accepting something does not mean you have to like it.

Accepting others is hard when they do not agree with you. **Practice** can make acceptance easier.

Key Word

Practice: do something over and over again to get better at it.

How Can You Learn to Be More Accepting?

Think about what you can and cannot control. Do not try to change the things you cannot control.

Think about how you would want to be treated if you were someone else. Then treat others how you would want to be treated.

How Can You Help Others Be More Accepting?

Be kind to others when they are upset. Do not tell them to get over it or that something is not a big deal. Let others feel their feelings.

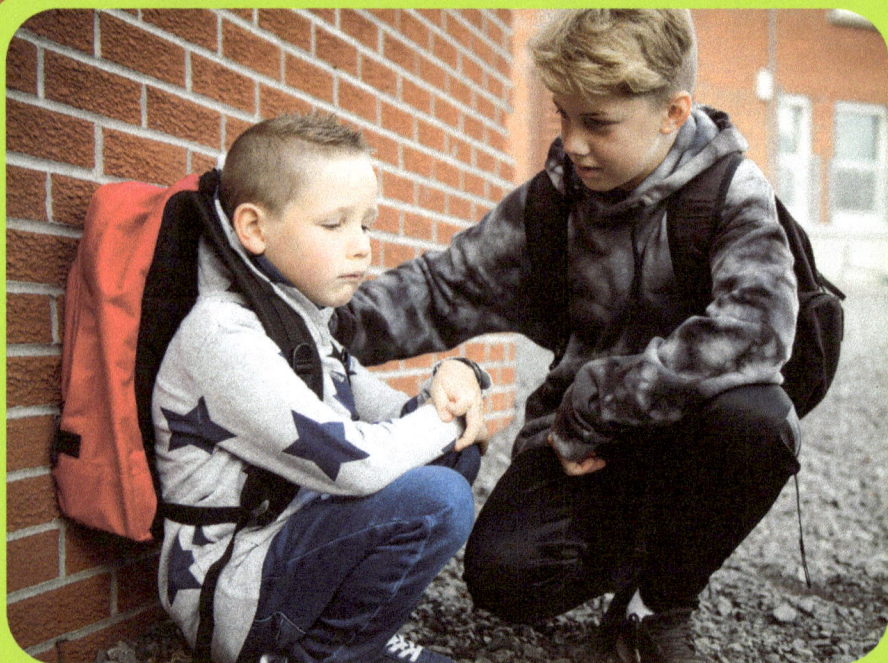

Teach others to be accepting by showing them what it looks like. Be okay with other people's differences.

How to Be Accepting Every Day

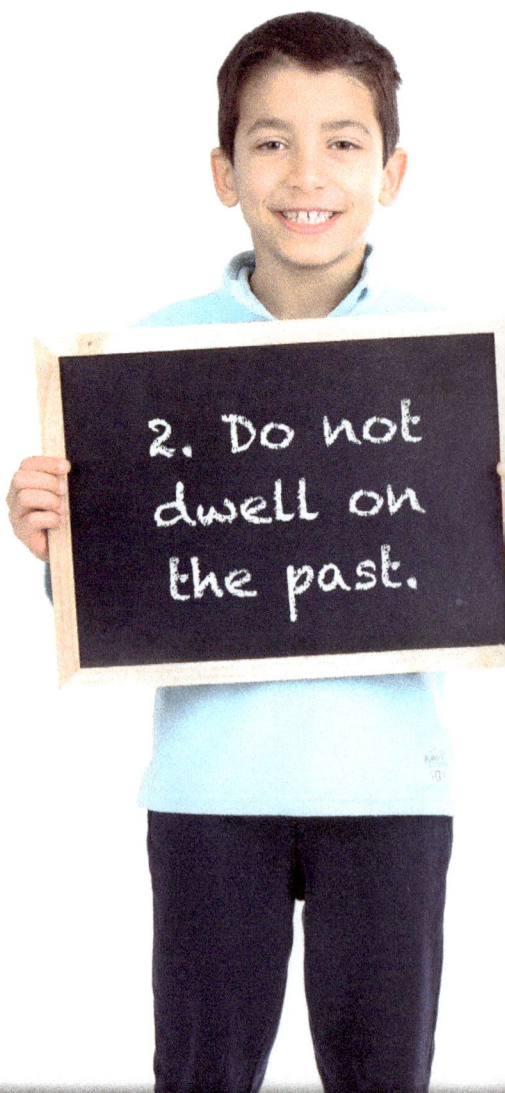

1. Give yourself time to feel your feelings.

2. Do not dwell on the past.

Key Word

Exclude: to keep someone or something out.

3. Do not exclude others.

4. Listen when others speak.

Acceptance Around the World

Death is a part of life. It is hard for people to lose a loved one. It brings up a lot of big feelings.

People who have lost a loved one have to accept their feelings. This helps them accept what happened. This acceptance helps them move forward with life.

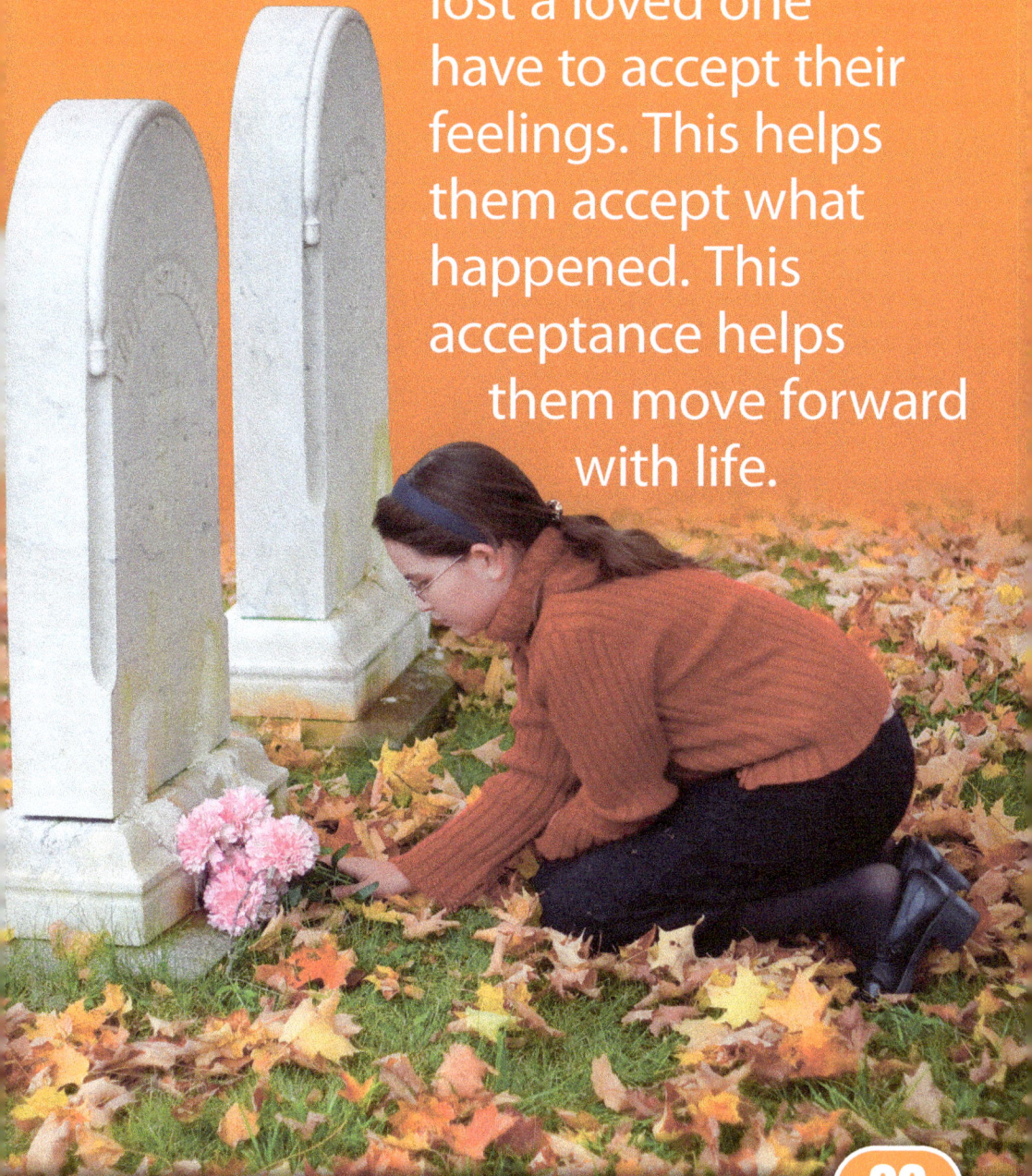

Quiz

Test your knowledge of acceptance by answering the following questions. The questions are based on what you have read in this book. The answers are listed on the bottom of the next page.

1 Does acceptance mean you have to be okay with someone's bad behavior?

2 Can pushing your feelings away make them stronger?

3 Does acceptance help you think about good things or bad things?

4 Should you always try to be accepting of other people?

5 Does accepting something mean you have to like it?

6 What should you not do to others?

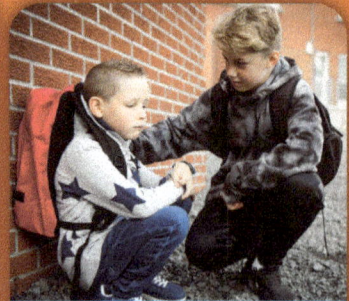

Explore Other Level 2 Readers.

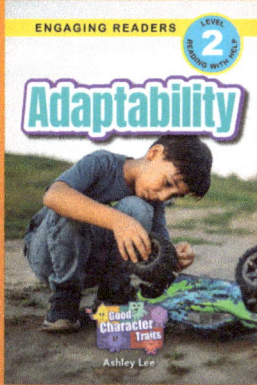
ENGAGING READERS — LEVEL 2 — READING WITH HELP
Adaptability
Good Character Traits
Ashley Lee

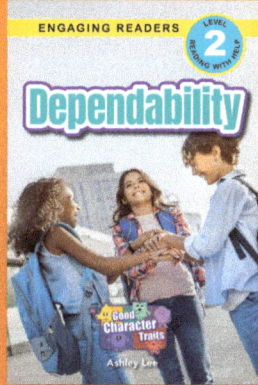
ENGAGING READERS — LEVEL 2 — READING WITH HELP
Dependability
Good Character Traits
Ashley Lee

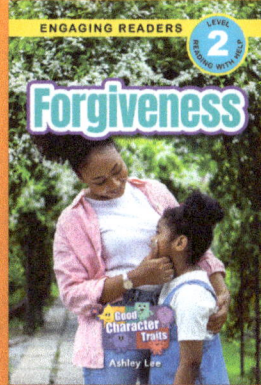
ENGAGING READERS — LEVEL 2 — READING WITH HELP
Forgiveness
Good Character Traits
Ashley Lee

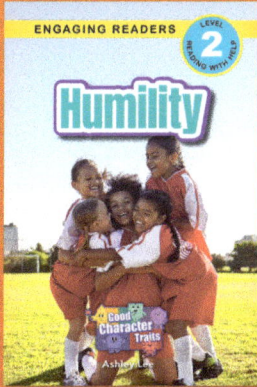
ENGAGING READERS — LEVEL 2 — READING WITH HELP
Humility
Good Character Traits
Ashley Lee

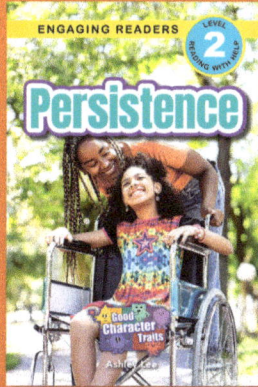
ENGAGING READERS — LEVEL 2 — READING WITH HELP
Persistence
Good Character Traits
Ashley Lee

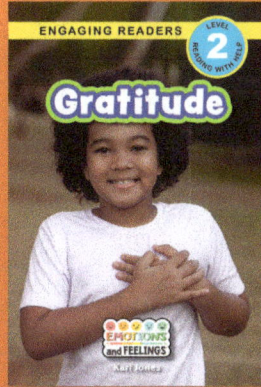
ENGAGING READERS — LEVEL 2 — READING WITH HELP
Gratitude
EMOTIONS and FEELINGS
Karl Jones

ENGAGING READERS — LEVEL 2 — READING WITH HELP
Grief
EMOTIONS and FEELINGS
Sarah Harvey

ENGAGING READERS — LEVEL 2 — READING WITH HELP
Love
EMOTIONS and FEELINGS
Sarah Harvey

ENGAGING READERS — LEVEL 2 — READING WITH HELP
Worry
EMOTIONS and FEELINGS
Sarah Harvey

Visit www.engagebooks.com/readers

Answers:
1. No 2. Yes 3. Good things 4. Yes 5. No 6. Exclude them

www.ingramcontent.com/pod-product-compliance
Lightning Source LLC
Chambersburg PA
CBHW052034030426
42337CB00027B/5008